BEI GRIN MACHT SICH IHR WISSEN BEZAHLT

- Wir veröffentlichen Ihre Hausarbeit,
  Bachelor- und Masterarbeit

- Ihr eigenes eBook und Buch -
  weltweit in allen wichtigen Shops

- Verdienen Sie an jedem Verkauf

Jetzt bei www.GRIN.com hochladen und kostenlos publizieren

GRIN

Amina Khalid, Aneeqa Zafar

A Study on L2 Teachers' beliefs about L1 in Pakistan

GRIN Verlag

Bibliografische Information der Deutschen Nationalbibliothek:

Die Deutsche Bibliothek verzeichnet diese Publikation in der Deutschen National-
bibliografie; detaillierte bibliografische Daten sind im Internet über http://dnb.d-
nb.de/ abrufbar.

Impressum:

Copyright © 2014 GRIN Verlag GmbH
Druck und Bindung: Books on Demand GmbH, Norderstedt Germany
ISBN: 978-3-656-91247-7

Dieses Buch bei GRIN:

http://www.grin.com/de/e-book/292990/a-study-on-l2-teachers-beliefs-about-l1-in-
pakistan

GRIN - Your knowledge has value

Der GRIN Verlag publiziert seit 1998 wissenschaftliche Arbeiten von Studenten, Hochschullehrern und anderen Akademikern als eBook und gedrucktes Buch. Die Verlagswebsite www.grin.com ist die ideale Plattform zur Veröffentlichung von Hausarbeiten, Abschlussarbeiten, wissenschaftlichen Aufsätzen, Dissertationen und Fachbüchern.

Besuchen Sie uns im Internet:

http://www.grin.com/

http://www.facebook.com/grincom

http://www.twitter.com/grin_com

A Study on L2 Teachers' beliefs about L1 in Pakistan

Amina Khalid
Aneeqa Zafar

A Study on L2 Teachers' beliefs about L1 in Pakistan

Please note: The author is not a native speaker.

Abstract:-

The purpose of the study is to find strategies used by teachers, to teach L2, to school level and university level students. The Data is collected from 50 teachers of different schools and universities of Lahore, Pakistan. The procedure for analysis is Hermeneutical Analysis. The study reveals that teachers use strategies according to the needs of students. Most of the Students came from different backgrounds and cultures, so they had no knowledge of L2, so, it was better to teach them difficult concepts in their native language. This study would make some contribution for teachers to know about strategies to teach students.

Keywords:

Native language, Second Language, Teaching Strategies.

Table of Contents

1. *Introduction*

In the end of 19th century direct method in language teaching class is used which ends the use of mix languages in language teaching class (Crook, 2001). From this point the word code-switching arouses. Native language is used in class but its use is limited in language class. This change raises many questions. Which function of native language should be used in class? Which language should not to use? Where code-switching is used and where not to use? As we know in Pakistan less attention is given to bilingual classrooms and now it's time to give more attention to this area. Therefore, the purpose if the paper was to explore teachers' belief about use of L1 in Language Teaching Class. Which language is preferred? Why it is important and how it will affect the students for learning L2?

1.1 Literature Review:

There are several researchers who have shed light on the use of L1 in foreign language classrooms in their works. The present study further explores new facets in this area.

Gulzar (2010) asserts that teachers frequently move back and forth between L1 and L2 while changing the topic. They employ L1 partially or fully while repeating the previously uttered sentences to make the students understand fully. He further posits that English language teachers in Pakistan are the native speakers of Urdu, Sindhi, Punjabi, Balochi, Pashto, etc. Sometimes teachers lack competence in target language and cannot recall the required word in target language, in such situations; they have to use the vocabulary of L1.

Tariq, Bilal, Abdas and Mahmood (2013) postulate that teachers employ L1 in the foreign language classroom to create a friendly environment. Socializing with students in their mother tongue, motivate them and outcomes will be in the form of their positive results.

Pablo, Lengeling, Zenil Crawford and Goodwin (2011) are of the view that teachers utilize L1 according to their students' language level. The frequency of first language use varies from beginning level to higher. Teaching L2 at the beginning level requires more use of mother tongue whereas there is a less use of L1 at higher level.

Kayaoglue (2012) opines that teachers employ the mother tongue of the students while teaching grammatical rules of the target language particularly in the beginning level.

While shedding light on another reason because of which teachers switch back to L2 learners' mother tongue, Edstrom (2009) posits that teachers utilize L1 when students get confused and are unable to understand the concepts in the target language so they need clarification. To clarify the concepts, teachers use their mother tongue on the part of target language.

Mufeed and Hasan (2010) put forward that using L1 for the purpose of translating difficult terms and grammatical points of foreign language is essential. When teachers employ translation, L2 learners also become able to notice the differences and similarities between their mother tongue and FL.

While sharing the point of view of Mufeed et al. (2010), Gomathi and Kiruthika (2013) assert that when L2 learners face difficulties in understanding the vocabulary items, teachers utilize translation as a pedagogical tool to make them understand. They translate the vocabulary of target language into their mother tongue. So L2 learners feel less nervous.

Meyer (2008) opines that students who are diffident get upset and frustrated in the environment of language classroom when they are unable to understand fully so teachers employ code-switching to make learning meaningful. Use of students' mother tongue proves helpful in making foreign language classroom a more comprehensible place and such sort of environment assist to lower affective filters.

Nation (2001) is of the view that use of mother tongue in foreign language classrooms is effective without any doubt but it should be only employed when it is needed and also should not be overdriven. Overutilization of L2 may affect gravely the L2 learners' performance in achieving their goals of proficiency in target language. So it should be used moderately.

1.2 Significance:

The topic of Code-Switching has significant role in Teaching L2 now-a-days. This study is important because it will explain different views shared by teachers. As we know, little attention is giving to English in our academic areas this study will help to find out different methods use by teachers in classroom for English Language Teaching.

1.3 Research Questions:

In light of all the research supporting the use of the L1 in L2 classrooms, this study will attempt to answer the following questions:

1. Strategies used by the Teachers to teach L2 learners in classroom at school level?

2. Strategies used by the Teachers to teach L2 learners in classroom at University level?

3. Whether there is any difference in employing teaching strategies t school and university   level?

2. *Methodology:*

Research Method is a very critical part of a research because it directly influences our conclusion section. It is very important to choose a research method that can be used easily and is in limits on what researchers can do in a given time. The method used in this study is purely Qualitative.

2.1 Participants:

The Data is collected from 50 different Teachers, teaching L2 at Primary-level and University level both male and female participants are involved in this study. All participants are considered to be highly skilled users of English language.

2.2 Data Collection:

The data was collected and analysed through qualitative method. Interviews are used as a tool for the collection of data. Structured Interview was set for the study. The main purpose of the structured interviews, which were based on a set of questions prepared in advance (see Appendix A & B), was to gain insight into the instructors' pedagogical perspective related to classroom English use. The interviews were recorded and also note-taking method is used for data collection based on the ease of the Participants.

2.3 Data Analysis:

As Morrill et al (2000) stated this study also have an emic focus rather than etic focus because this will focus on the data given by the participants and their viewpoints rather of the data the research given.

This study is analysed by using Hermeneutical Analysis. According to an article "Hermeneutics" by "N.Froster" Hermeneutics means the theory of Interpretation, i.e. it's the theory which helps in gaining the understanding of texts, utterances etc. It deals with the nature of interpretation its scope and significance and is very much in use now-a-days. It connects with language direct and interpretation of the text.

3. *Findings or results:*

The Findings of first question that is Strategies used by the Teachers to teach L2 learners in classroom at school level are:

Participants	Q1	Q2	Q3	Q4	Q5
1	Only English is used in classroom. Focus is only on English Language	While teaching difficult concepts code-switching is used	Obviously both languages will effect	Use code-switching to give complete concept about things. Especially in story classes for pre-school students.	L1 helps to develop strong concepts about target language.
2	Preferred to use English but based on students' needs	Use L1 for explaining difficult concepts.	By using L1 in class it kills the importance of L2 language.	Use code-switching when students don't understand the concepts and to make those concepts clear teacher use code-	L1 helps in different ways but most students come from different background, schools, families so for them L2 is

7

				switching.	difficult to understand so in these cases L1 helps them.
3	L1 should be used in classrooms because Pre-school students are not aware of English language more.	L1 is preferred because students will understand difficult things more clearly with their native language.	By using L1 in class didn't affect the target language. It will help in attaining goals in target language.	Use code-switching in class while explaining difficult concepts because most students are faint they didn't get the message in full form.	L1 is a helping tool because students came from different environment and English is difficult for them because they have less vocabulary.
4	L1 should be used. Sometimes have to use to convey message but	No L1 is used they are motivated to use L2. Use simpler vocabulary	L1 will not affect L2. It is based on in which level they are. For	Code-switching is used while explain difficult concepts or	L1 is helping tool it is used and helpful sometimes to understand meaning. To

	it's the least choice for them.	while explaining difficult concepts.	beginners L1 is used only. GTM method is used.	have no background of L2 at all.	get feedback can be in L1 but motivated to participate in class.
5	Most of the time try to use English but is according to needs of students.	While explain difficult concepts L1 is used.	Yes, use of L1 will prevent in attaining goals of target language.	When continuously use L2 students get bored or didn't understand context fully so this situation use code-switching.	L1 is helping tool in Direct Translation method.
6	L1 is used but try to use L2 more in classroom.	For understand of students L1 is used to explain difficult concepts.	Definitely, L1 will effect L2 but its base on level of motivation whether teacher encourage or	Mostly students are from different backgrounds so for purpose of their understanding use code-switching.	L1 should be the first priority. Use Direct Translation method. So L1 is helping tool in this case.

			discourage while using L2.		
7	Management prefer to use L2 more.	Based on knowledge of students eg:- in class of 20 students 10 are getting the meaning and 10 are not then use L1 to explain the difficult concepts.	It will affect but force them to use L2 more.	Use code-switching when students didn't get the main points. Motivate to use L2.	L1 help but its depend on students' ability to attain any language.

The Findings of second question that is Strategies used by the Teachers to teach L2 learners in classroom at university level are:

Participants	Q 1	Q2	Q3	Q4	Q5
1	Yes, it is used to some extent.	At first teacher explain in L2, but then, to make sure all students have understood, they explain it in L1 too.	If L1 is used wisely, and only, if necessary, it helps students to grasp the difficult concepts and does not hamper L2 learning.	When dealing with literature based material.	For language teaching it should be avoided.
2	Yes, because students come from all over the Pakistan and some of them do not understand fully in L2.	First, lecture is delivered in L2 then it is repeated in L1 for better understanding.	No, it does not.	Sometimes code switching is used for teacher's own ease. Considering different backgrounds of students, mixing different	Urdu as a medium of instruction in English language classroom sounds weird.

				languages and giving examples in different languages from different culture would enhance possibility of same concept.	
3	Yes, mother tongue is always a more suitable way of communication to make the concepts clearer.	L1 is always preferred when students face difficulty in understanding the difficult concepts.	L1 should not be allowed in Language classrooms.	Sometimes code switching occurs for emphasis and repetition.	If students lack the awareness about the new terminology then it can be allowed otherwise it should be discouraged.
4	Yes, teacher has to use L1.	Teacher should try his/her best to	Yes, it does affect students'	To make the environment of class	In language class rooms, teacher

		stay on L2. He or She can use easy vocabulary and simple sentence structure.	performance in learning L2.	friendly and to give example from the students' culture in their mother tongue for better understanding.	should try her/his best to avoid L1. He can use other strategies to make the students understand.
5	Not exactly depends on which language is used as a medium of instruction for students. Mostly English is used at university level.	L2 is preferred is classroom but sometimes students face difficulty in understanding concepts so switch to L1 for ease of students.	L1 is not allowed in classroom it is only used by teachers to explain difficult concepts.	L1 is used when students can't be able to attain the goals. L1 is used only for this purpose.	L1 is not using as a tool any more. In today's society L2 is used as a primary language. So more importance is given to L2.

The results of third question that is whether there is any difference in employing teaching strategies at school and university level are:

Interview Questions	School Level Findings	University Level findings
Q1: Is Urdu as L1 used in English language classrooms	Not exactly is in use. But sometimes it is used according to students' needs.	Yes, because students come from all over the Pakistan and some of them do not understand fully in L2. And mother tongue is always a more suitable way of communication to make the concepts clearer.
Q2: L1 or L2, which language is preferred in the language classrooms by teachers while explaining difficult concepts to the students	Code-switching is used while explaining difficult concepts but preferred to use simple vocabulary for students' understanding.	Both language are preferred first lecture is given in L2 then to make sure students get the concepts repeats the lecture in L1
Q3: If using L1 is allowed in the language classrooms, does it prevent students from attaining the goal in target language	Use of L1 in L2 class will affect the target language because it kills the importance of target language.	L1 in not allowed to use in class but If L1 is used wisely it helps students to grasp the difficult concepts and does not hamper L2 learning.
Q4: In which	Use code-switching when	Code-switching is used to give

14

situations and for what purposes, teachers use code switching in classrooms	students don't understand the concepts and to make those concepts clear teacher use code-switching.	examples of different culture to students of different background. And to make sure they grasp the idea completely.
Q5: How do you justify, L1 as a learning tool for L2 learners at school level?	L1 help to attain goals in target language. Because it gives complete concept about things which ones' can't be understand in L2. So it's a learning tool for L2 learners.	Today L1 is not used as a learning tool. L1 is avoided to use in classrooms so it is not use a learning tool in todays' society.

4. *Discussion*

Teachers tend to use direct method to motivate their students and to refrain the students from using native language and only use target language in classroom which help them to attain target language easily. Teachers motivate them to speak L2 and so students speak L2 in the language classroom which helps them to learn the language quickly. Another strategy is, the use of grammar-translation method, in which students first learn grammatical rules and then apply these rules by translating sentences to and from target language. Mostly teachers use this method at school level especially in story reading classes in which for students' ease teachers translate the story in their native language. The purpose of using this method is to clear main idea of the story. So, it will help the students to get the whole concept easily and it will also increase students' vocabulary. Teachers employ Scaffolding, because when students face difficulty in any task, teachers provide the appropriate support to them, it gives them enough of a "boost" to achieve the task. By giving help step by step students get motivate to learn more and more.

5. *Conclusion*

The presents study explored the teachers' contentions about the use of mother tongue of L2 learners in the language classroom by employing the qualitative research methodology. Hermeneutical analysis that is called the theory of interpretation is used for the analysis of L2 instructors' pedagogical perspectives related to language classrooms at university level as well as school level.

The findings reveal that teachers both at university level and school level utilize direct method, grammar translation method and the technique of scaffolding while teaching to the L2 learners in the language classrooms. By making all these methods and techniques a kingpin, it is probed in this research work that employing direct method really helps the L2 learners to learn the target language easily and rapidly. By taking into account the importance of L1 as a learning tool, some teachers take help from L2 learners' mother tongue, so they use grammar translation method. While some educators utilize the technique of scaffolding in language classroom where they provide the help to L2 learners where they need.

There are many precursory researches that have been conducted in this area but the present study particularly draws attention towards the importance of mother tongue while teaching to the L2 learners in the language classrooms. The present study would proffer the ground to further explore that how teachers can overcome the sociolinguistic barriers while teaching to L2 learners in a multilingual setting.

References

Ahmad, B. H. & Jusoff, K. (2009). Teachers' code-switching in classroom instructions for low English proficient learners. English Language Teaching.

Afzal Shehzad,(2013). *Using of the first language in english classroom as a way of scaffolding for the both students and teachers to learn and teach English,* University of Iran. Science Explorer Publications.

Cook, V. (2001). Second language learning and teaching. New York: Oxford University Press

Edstrom, A. M. (2009). Teacher reflection as a strategy for evaluating L1/L2 use in the classroom. *Babylonia, 1*(09).

GOMATHI, B., & KIRUTHIKA, P. Role of L1 in English Language Teaching To Rural Area Students with Reference To Erode Region.

Gulzar, M. A. (2010). Code-switching: Awareness about its utility in bilingual classrooms. *Bulletin of Education and Research, 32*(2), 23-44.

Jadallah, M., & Hasan, F. (2010, October). A review of some new trends in using L1 in the EFL classroom. In *National Conference on:" Improving TEFL Methods & Practices at Palestinian Universities.*

Kayaoğlu, M. N. (2012). The use of mother tongue in foreign language teaching from teachers" practice and perspective. *Pamukkale Üniversitesi Eğitim Fakültesi Dergisi, 32,* 25-35.

Latysanyphone Soulignavong,(2009). Using L1 in Teaching Vocabulary to low English Proficiency level students: A case study at the National University of Laos.

Meyer, H. (2008). The pedagogical implications of L1 use in the L2 classroom.*Maebashi Kyoai Gakuen College Ronsyu, 8*, 147-159.

Mora Pablo, I., Lengeling, M. M., Rubio Zenil, B., Crawford, T., & Goodwin, D. (2011). Students and teachers' reasons for using the first language within the foreign language classroom (French and English) in Central Mexico. *Profile Issues in Teachers Professional Development, 13*(2), 113-129.

N. Froster Micheal,(2001). *Hermeneutics,* University of Chicago Press.

Nation, P. (2003). The role of the first language in foreign language learning.*Asian EFL Journal, 5*(2), 1-8.

Pie-Shi Wing, (2009). *Code switching as a strategy use in EFL classroom in Taiwan,* Tankang University, Taiwan.

Tariq, A. R., Bilal, H. A., Abbas, N., & Mahmood, A. (2013). Functions of Code-switching in Bilingual Classrooms. *Research on Humanities and Social Sciences, 3*(14), 29-34.

Appendix A

Terms: L1- Urdu Language

      L2- English Language

      Code switching – Mixture of both L1 and L2 in conversation.

Q1: Is Urdu as L1 used in English language classrooms at school level in Pakistan?

Q2: L1 or L2, which language is preferred in the language classrooms by teachers while explaining difficult concepts to the students at school level?

Q3: If using L1 is allowed in the language classrooms, does it prevent students from attaining the goal in target language at school level?

Q4: In which situations and for what purposes, teachers use code switching in classrooms at school level?

Q5: How do you justify, L1 as a learning tool for L2 learners at school level?

Appendix B

Terms: L1- Urdu Language

L2- English Language

Code switching – Mixture of both L1 and L2 in conversation.

Q1: Is Urdu as L1 used in English language classrooms at university level in Pakistan?

Q2: L1 or L2, which language is preferred in the language classrooms by teachers while explaining difficult concepts to the students at university level?

Q3: If using L1 is allowed in the language classrooms, does it prevent students from attaining the goal in target language at university level?

Q4: In which situations and for what purposes, teachers use code switching in classrooms at university level?

Q5: How do you justify, L1 as a learning tool for L2 learners at university level?